Available Light

Available Light

Poems

Sandy Coomer

Iris Press
Oak Ridge, Tennessee

Cover Photo: "Hidden Lake" by Jordan Steranka
Instagram: @jordansteranka

Book Design: Robert B. Cumming, Jr.

Iris Press
www.irisbooks.com

Library of Congress Cataloging-in-Publication Data

Names: Coomer, Sandy, 1963- author.
Title: Available light : poems / Sandy Coomer.
Description: Oak Ridge, Tennessee : Iris Press, [2019]
Identifiers: LCCN 2019006239 | ISBN 9781604542561 (pbk. : alk. paper)
Classification: LCC PS3603.O57974 A6 2019 | DDC 811/.6—dc23
LC record available at https://lccn.loc.gov/2019006239

Acknowledgments

Grateful thanks and appreciation to the following journals within which these poems first appeared, sometimes in slightly different forms.

Anomaly Literary Journal: "The Minotaur's Last Interview"
BlazeVOX: "My Name is…," "I Won't Call This a Love Poem," "The First Time I Ate Oysters," and "Postcard to my Father from the Mojave Desert"
CEO Literary Magazine: "Love Poem"
Euphemism: "Tattoo"
Firefly Magazine: "Night in June"
Flycatcher Journal: "The Chicken House"
Forage: "There"
Gnarled Oak: "Frost Flowers"
The Hunger: "Sun and Rain"
The Hungry Chimera: "Keep the Hand Moving"
Hypertrophic Literary Magazine: "How We Fit"
The Inflectionist Review: "Unknowing" (Fragment)
Lindenwood Review: "Pentimento"
Mojave Heart Journal: "Letter to Andrew from Flagstaff," "The Silence," "Hypnosis by Landscape"
Mud Season Review: "Kitchen," "Calligraphy," and "The Small Book of Virtues"
The Noctua Review: "Letter to Debbie from the Lincoln Park Zoo"
Number One: "Morning"
Oyster River Pages: "Available Light," "Between Us," and "Visit from my Lost Child"
Phoenix Soul: "Austin"
POEM: "Memorial for Stephanie"
Ristau: A Journal of Being: "An Ending" and "Postcard to Shelley from Sanibel Island"
River and South Review: "Advice"
Rose Red Review: "The Sex Life of Swans"
Sheila-Na-Gig Online: "Anniversary," "Stillborn," "Child on a Balcony," "On Hold," "Letter to Beth from Vermont," and "Letter to Victoria from Monteagle Mountain"
Streetlight Press: "At the Retreat, We Reflect on our Intentions" and "Postcard to Laura from Eureka Springs"

Through the Gate: "Pomegranate"

Treehouse, An Exhibition of the Arts: "Religion"

Tule Review: "How a Woman Learns to Sing the Coyote's Song" (published as "Welfare Office")

Wildflower Muse: "My Father is the Poem I'll Never Write" and "Split"

WINK: Writers in the Know: "Loving a Dying Man"

Contents

IV. THE DARK LAKE

V. WHATEVER LIGHT LIES WAITING

VI. THE LIGHT BRILLIANT AND ENDLESS

For Shawn,
whose beautiful light never fails

with much love

Someone I loved once gave me
a box full of darkness.

It took me years to realize
that this, too, was a gift.

—Mary Oliver

•

Language is light. Or else language is another atmosphere,
through which light or its analog travels, diffuses, spreads.

—Allison Boyd Justus

I.

A Balance of Shadows

Religion

As morning bees spring brightly,
I watch the day
unwind from the coil of night.

I step around a web of threads
woven into the shape of an eye,
open and glistening.

The grass carries the burden
of my footprints the same way
my skin knows touch.

I am as close to love as I allow
myself to be. My softest whispers
turn it like a wheel.

I can't rid myself
of this clumsy body, this needy skin,
so I sink my toes in dirt. I run in rain.

I breathe the scent of honeysuckle
and sun on a rock like a salamander,
lazy and blinking.

I don't know which words to pray,

but I can cup a firefly in my hand
and watch it crawl to my fingertip
before it lifts its light to the swirling dark.

The Chicken House

for my grandmother

So you would not have to live with the in-laws,
you trudged the field to the two room shack
that once held chickens, and before that tobacco,
in its stale rafters. A bucket of water, a rag, and a broom
made the chicken house a home with its narrow porch,
kitchen with kerosene stove where you cooked beans
and potatoes, and bedroom with a stone fireplace.

In the summer, the ice man, with iron tongs,
plunked a chunk of ice for the chest. In winter,
snowflakes shimmied through the cracks in the roof
and you'd catch them on your tongue. You churned
butter on the porch and listened to mockingbirds fuss
while the breeze built a storm above the tobacco fields
and lifted the scent of chickens from the gray boards.

The in-laws called you stubborn, as raindrops splattered
in every pot and pan, as dirt collected in cracks, and mice
gathered beneath floorboards. But you would say your nest
was as good as a palace as you flopped beside your husband
in the creaky bed. The crickets waxed their violins as clouds
spread harmonic against the moon's molten glow, as love,
in its grand simplicity, strummed a tune on the clothesline.

Child on a Balcony

Back streets always have eyes
and yours hold the morning open.

A tightrope of space
on your tiny balcony, you grip

the bars with fingers straight
from your mouth, the lick

and taste of your world.
Will you remember me,

my American wave, and how
my pause gave you permission

to tuck your chubby face
behind your arms? You stayed

like the morning, a little longer
curdled into thought and became

an image I hold, its blushed moment
a fragment of focused faith.

Maybe you already see
this world is a balance of shadows

and what we claim as real
is only our version of truth.

Looking down, did you see the same
morning that I saw looking up,

and in that frame and capture, did I see
the same you as you will one day be?

Your dark umber eyes blink the future
awake. Wonder unfurls and washes

the soul-stung cobblestones
hobbled with grief.

What would this balcony be
without you but a sliver of rock

gripping an empty sleeve of space?
And what would I be but a woman

still restless, still looking up,
eyes searching, hands empty.

Snow Day

I climb the stairs
to wake my teenage son,
breathe
his sleepy warmth,
absorb the past
and its devotion.

I know the past is not
what I'm supposed to be
thinking of.
His future, in so many boxes,
waits to be opened
like the snow waits
for footprints
across the unmarked.

But I do think about the past.
We can't quite fit
in it anymore,
like his body along the bed's edge
can't quite fit.
His hair mashes against
his ear and his long bones
rest lanky, untethered.

I think about
breathing
and holding my breath,
holding it in—
all of this—
the snow
and his long slow
breaths and that I won't wake him
to tell him there's no school.

Today, I'll let him sleep
while the snow falls,
the blinding white wrapped
across the meadow
like skin.

Sea Turtles

I'm luckier than most, alone
every morning on the beach
while my mother feeds
my little sisters and her own
dark sorrows. It's made me
sure-footed, all that practice
walking the surf, so I can
stand in the ocean swells
and talk out the world's sins
with the gulls and sea shells
and small bits of green glass.
This early, there's nothing to do
but stare, and anyway,
mother says crying won't
get you anywhere and so far,
that's been true for me.

I find the marks where sea turtles
hatched and dragged their new
bodies through sand but they're
gone now, riding quiet on
the back of a dark quick tide.
I take a stick of driftwood
and write names of all the people
I love in one column
and all the people I think
will love me back in another
and the first column is longer
than the second, much longer.

I think of the sea turtles
and how after so long being
covered with sand, their shelled-up
hearts matching the rhythms

of their brothers, one bright night
they crawl new and lonely
and take their solace in the sea.
I guess in one way it's good to know
your place but in another way
if you know it too well it's hard
to dream for anything else, so now
I feel a little sorry for the turtles,
all alone in a watery world.

I line the bits of glass
between the names I wrote
and the sun catches green
on the edge of day. I think
if no one ever loves me back
I can love the world a little bit harder
and make up for it. Mother says
you have to earn trust and I guess
love's the same, so until I learn
how to earn, I have these mornings
and the arms of the sea to keep me
company. I imagine the baby turtles
calling out some secret code and finding
each other and it makes me happy
to think they won't be alone anymore.
The tide comes in and smooths
the names I wrote until they're gone
but I catch the bits of glass before
they wash away. I'll save them
for tomorrow.

The Secret of Sound

The words you say in confidence
to your best friend about what you did
behind the football stadium with Chris

will not end up raising someone's
eyebrows in a kitchen in Tupelo.
Even though every voice is as unique

as the body that produces it, the song
you sing in the shower cannot
incriminate you. Listen to the pitch and tone

of these words—how they fall with a singular
transparency. I'm not trying to impress
anyone with my intellect. I've been there,

like you, wondering if there's a solution
to sadness. When we're bottled up tight as a seed
in a hothouse flower, how do we unloose ourselves?

If inside every wooden bird there is a tree
that held other birds and their song
filtered down the ridge and woke a sleepy writer,

she might pout a little bit, pour coffee,
then scribble a line of love, then speak it aloud.
If that line finds its way somehow to the heart

of a lonely girl who at this moment is crying
in a car in the unlit corner of a Mini Mart parking lot,
listening to Led Zeppelin on the radio,

who's to say we aren't saving each other?

Morning

I leave you sleeping
in the quiet. The timid sun
hasn't yet reached the back porch
and purple-gray mist circles
the yard like castle walls. I wait
for last night's anger to reappear,
but it takes too much work
to dig it out of memory. I let it sink
into the recess of those things
that can't be explained,
let it sit with the cool dawn
that stills the flutter of what I
both hope for and fear.
I think if I stay here
and let the day form around me
I can be reborn with it. If we move
slower, we can catch up with each other.
If we're silent, we can hear the breath
that brought us together years ago.
We can hear the words we used
to say spring out of the air
that still holds them true.

Postcard to Shelley from Sanibel Island

I watch the water pull the sand,
and the sand cradle the water as it coughs
up a treasure—sea glass, a starfish,
some old piece of fabric that might once
have been part of a sail. At the edge
of the surf, I draw a line, then watch it
dissolve like your plans to get lost enough
to find yourself. You wandered for a year,
arriving at the places you needed to be,
staying until you needed to leave, sifting
words through your fingers like sunlight
through clouds. You held it in memory—
a pelican's clip of wing on wave, the shape
of a heart formed in rock, the scent of brine
and rotting fish. You are fluid, as much
as I am land-locked and stubborn, my hands
always needing to be filled. I want what's
certain, but you said nothing can be kept
except silence and discontent, and those
we can trade for paper and filtered light.
I watch sea gulls and wonder what they know
of loneliness, the kind you have to travel
far to escape. How much longer are you
willing to wander, Shelley? Tell me,
how much have you missed yourself?

Letter to Victoria from Monteagle Mountain

I breathe the bouquet of fireplace embers and distant storm.
Above me, footsteps tap across the 100-year-old pine floors
and someone talks on the phone—a happy lilting laugh,
then conversation steady as the stone bridge over the creek.

I am here to write but the words have yet to find me, twisting
as they do along the ridgetop and billowing like fog across
the hills. The pond carries a thin layer of ice and below it,
a carpet of lilies, the roots clutching to silt like fingers in sand.

Words sink and leaves settle—both blow bubbles to the oaks.
I recall how you told me to neither seek nor entice, but let
the morning open like prayer, let the words want so much to be
written that they climb through my hands like a wizard's spell.

For that, I have to be patient. For that, I have to sit cross-legged
on the floor like a child, rock the bones of my hips to a song
only the earth sings. You say be grounded, but what you mean
is to grind. I stir the spice of cumin and pepper, the veil of onion.

I collect eggshells for the compost pile, carrot skin and orange rind.
Deer gorge on chestnuts beside the dormant garden. I do yoga
on the porch, my toes slipping in new rain. I am waiting, Victoria,
as hard as I can.

Letter to Beth from Vermont

It's snowing again.
I asked a man in the laundromat
if it ever stops snowing in Vermont.
He said not this week, and we watch
our flannel shirts and wool socks spin.
Snow makes me lonely, all the white
space of it, the blank page I want
to crush with my fur-lined boots.
I'm not made for this cold, so heavy
and silent, like the black wing that
now masks your face. You used
to sing. Your words used to spark
the wild tangle in both of us until
your tongue was clipped and you
trembled in the dark. I told you
to live for love and love betrayed you,
swallowed the sweet curve of your hand
like an owl gulps mice. I told you
to live for joy and joy let you chase it
for a while, then folded its arms
and fell asleep. What can I tell you then
about this snow that you'll believe
except that when I step outside and sink
to my knees, it's a kind of prayer
that holds me up. When I blink
the whiteness back to color, I see
what's clean and possible, a field un-
broken, the curved crest of frosted hills.
Don't worry if this note arrives damp
or the ink smeared. I added a handful
of snow to the envelope so you can see
what I see—all the beautiful crystals
laid out flat in your palm.

Keep the Hand Moving

is the first rule of free writing
but I would rather hold my hands
together, fingertips touching,
and speak affirmations like
I am beautiful,
trying hard to believe it, trying
to blot out the voice in my head
that says *You know better than that*
or *You've got to be joking.*
I would rather open my hands
and see what falls into them—
feathers or leaves
or sunlight glinting off a tin roof.

But the rule says, move.
That's the language of effort
and the checkmarks we pen
on our lists go down, then up,
in a sort of frenzy.
I am all about frenzy
and fresh air and French kissing
but that's hardly the point here,
though I think there's always
a point to kissing. The hand
is sensuous, long and delicate,
the bones fragile, yet strong
enough to write a thousand words
one after another, in a sensible order,
so that when they are read aloud
they sound a lot like
We are all so beautiful.

II.

THE VOICELESS SKY

At the Retreat, We Reflect on our Intentions

A thought stands
in the tall green grass beside my bed
and with a thin, well-carved hand, motions
for me to follow. I live in dreams, so this is not unusual
except for its flower dress, a camouflage for the wide fields,
and its river tongue spilling blue feathers on the sheets.
It slips a bracelet around my wrist and asks me to
count the wooden beads. They twist like minutes
in an hour. I wish I could repeat myself.
I need the practice.

I need to practice
repeating myself each hour,
counting wooden beads like minutes.
I slip a bracelet around my wrist and I am made
a river tongue, spilling blue feathers on the sheets.
Except for a flowery dress, my camouflage in the wide fields,
I am, I think, a dream. This is not unusual.
My thin, well-carved hand motions
in the green grass beside my bed
where once a thought stood.

Eve Finds Adam Asleep in the Garden

It is good not to be alone, but if alone she must be,
Eve will scratch the earth and bloom herself to life.

All the wild animals and the birds in the sky
watch her gather water, furrow the soil, space the seeds.

She names them leopard and giraffe, flamingo
and mourning dove. She sends them forth

according to their nature, to roam the earth
and settle in a place that affords their passions—

gray squirrel to the mighty oak, copperhead to canyon deep,
ostrich to dry savannah. And the man she finds sleeping

with the wound in his side, she will call Lover
after she stitches his flesh closed with her hair

and carries water in her hands to bathe his fevered face.
He calls her Helpmate, and Soft Eyes, and Mine,

but she tells him she is her own as she helps him up
from the sleeping place to harvest the green lettuces,

the orange peppers, to trample the olives into oil,
the grapes into wine. Eve feels no shame,

the sun glazing the muscles of her thighs, her back.
They work together. She sees that, for now, it is good.

My Name is…

When the barista at Starbucks, poised with pen against cup,
asked me my name, I looked into his coffee-brown eyes
and said Agnes—
just like that. And, just like that, he wrote it
in bold capital letters and went about brewing and pouring
while I pondered why Agnes had come out of my mouth
with no pre-thought or planning and the many times
I wanted to be someone else
but not Agnes,
though it's as fine a name as any.

Once, I knew a girl named Meadow
and another named River
and I wished I had said one of those names, or maybe
chosen the name of one of my mother's high school friends
whose parents labeled all the girls after the states
they were born in—Tennessee, Alabama, Kentucky—
strong names with a sense of where they'd been
and where they were going.

While I contemplated who I might be
the next time I ordered a Mocha Lite Frappuccino,
the barista nodded his head, said
Agnes
and the way he said it, drawn out with feeling,
sexy even, the syllables floating above the music
and conversation, made the whole shop stop
to see who this Agnes was—
we all waited for Agnes to take her drink,
all of us together waited,
while the barista stared with his coffee eyes
and with a startled *Oh,*
I remembered it was me.

Selfie

I walk past a large clean shop window,
catch my reflection and stop.
I am not the beauty I imagine myself to be.
My skin is sallow and my eyes fatigued.
I can do nothing about my hair or my hips.

My mother always said to finish every outfit
with a smile. If you don't feel like smiling, fake it.
All this smiling stuff is hard for the serious-minded,
for the mouth that curves downward with contemplation.
Some hearts are heavy, some souls are old, or maybe,
as my mother suggests, I just think too much.

My daughter taught me the best way to take selfies.
Hold the phone above you, she said, and tilt your face
toward the light so that shadows don't sag your eyes.
I lift my chin and grin. I can't find a good angle
in the sun glinting off the shop window.
My smile comes off more like a wince.

I straighten my back, suck in my belly, and realize
I'm attracting attention. Workers on the other side
of the street stare at me. The woman inside the shop,
whose window I've commandeered, inches toward
the phone. I'm concerned she's calling the cops
but I can't stop now.

I drop my shopping bags and take off my jacket,
turn sideways to judge my profile. I summon
a model's grace but it comes off strained, unnatural.
I slump against the window as the woman inside
rises from her stool to wave me away.

I flash her a smile before I go.

On Hold

after Amy Gerstler

Press one if you'd like to go back to Kindergarten and tell Mrs. Kirksey that you *did* know how to draw a triangle, and you *could* pick out orange from the box of crayons, you just didn't want to.

Press two if you want to back flip to 7th grade and tell Kristen Merriweather that you'd rather be dragged by wild horses through a gully filled with rattlesnakes than go to her party.

Press three if you want to take your virginity back from the boy you gave it to, wrap it in silver and purple striped paper, and leave it as a surprise gift for the person you really love.

Press four if winter makes you lonely and you'd like to hear a recording of "Kokomo" by the Beach Boys.

Press five for chocolate and wine to be auto-delivered to your house every week.

Press six for your grandparents to un-die, for your parents to un-divorce and for your dog to get un-hit by a car so that you can all enjoy another 4th of July picnic together with hotdogs, corn-on-the-cob and watermelon.

Press seven for instructions on how to lift blood stains from carpet, candle wax from bed sheets or chewing gum from hair.

Press eight for directions on how to dissolve your insecurities in vinegar and baking soda.

Press nine to hear this list again.

Press zero for Operator, but don't expect anyone to answer.

Interview Question #1: Can you tell me about yourself?

I have green eyes, not blue, though people say they look blue.
    I'm a perfectionist.
I wake in the middle of the night laughing at my dreams.
    I wake in the middle of the night with a rush of fear,
    like a candle blown out, the tail of smoke drifting.
I wish I believed in ghosts.
    If I believed in ghosts I would like them
    better than crowds.
I like following a trail to its end, no matter how long it takes.
    I don't like writing in a diary. I don't reminisce.
I like books. I like fires.
    I can drink coffee late at night. Sugar makes me jumpy.
I like silence better than noise.
    I drink too much wine. I've been so drunk I let
    a man take advantage of me, but it wasn't with wine,
    and it wasn't really taking advantage.
I am a runner. I have ugly feet. Sometimes I cry when I run.
    Running is beautiful.
I am tempted to attempt skydiving.
    I like speed, but not being upside-down or underwater.
I'm fascinated by birds. Fish, not so much.
    I've considered ways to commit suicide, not that I
    wanted to do it, but just in case it ever came to that.
I am not, at all, afraid of blood.
    I am afraid of water.
I'm enamored with tattoos. The poet, Gregory Pardlo, wrote
"Tattoos are like children; have one, you'll want another."
    I filled six spiral notebooks with poems.
When I read them, they made my throat thick.
    I burned them in a circle I drew with a stick.
    It was a blaze of words. It was a one match fire.
Sometimes I feel my heartbeat in my eyes.
    My heart is a plum. My heart is a bloom of jasmine.
    My heart is a shark's tooth.

At my other job, the manager said he hired me because
I was beautiful.
>He didn't see the quiet in me, only what he hoped
>was a bracelet of heat.
I daydream a lot, but I wouldn't if I got this job. I would never
daydream at work.
>I am a loner, but not at work. I work well with others.
Is this enough?
>Did I give you what you wanted?

Interview Question #2: Where are you from?

I'm from my mother's belly. She pushed me out
with her bright heart wailing. I matched her cries with my own.
I'm from my father's anger, his red face twisting like a vine.
I'm from the middle of three sisters, each of us pressing
bruises into skin and passing the purple hue to the sunset
over the mountains. I'm from the no-good dirt, the voiceless sky,
the black wing of a crow, the leg of a wolf caught in a trap.
Call me southerner, call me plain, call me witness,
that's where I'm from. I struck out on my own,
saw the train coming and held my breath. I'm smoke and smite,
the bright trill of the whistle and the blink of the crossties.
I'm the empty pocket, the canned vegetables, powdered milk.
I'm from the vacant barn I slipped into, the dirt floor I fell to
with a boy named David. I'm from the mouths we pressed together.
I'm from the ash heap of burned journals, the words too dangerous
to keep. I'm from the careful circle drawn with a stick
that kept those ashes safe. I'm from the sidewalk,
and a night too empty for tears. I'm from the twin bed
I kneeled beside, whispering prayers I thought might take me far
from where I'm from. They didn't, and I'm still here.

Postcard to Laura from Eureka Springs

The Ozarks push outward
and upward and on the ledge
this town clings like ivy. They say
water from the springs will heal
and when I ask what ailment exactly,
they answer everything from arthritis
to blindness. Should I throw myself in,
dear Laura, the way we cannonballed
from the diving board at the YMCA pool,
immerse my body in magic
so that you can touch my skin
and be healed too? I walk the broken
sidewalk to the shops on Spring Street—
Sailor's Luck Tattoo, Crystal Water Beads,
Scarlett's Lingerie and Curiosities—
and wish you were here to drag me
into the Mystic Moon Psychic Shop
and buy tarot cards and deal our future
out in front of us. What would we find,
Laura, but a ribbon of longing
which we'd pull from our throats
and wear around our wrists like scars.
You were afraid to want too much,
but I want to believe the future
can taste like ginger, like almonds,
and can heal our ruined bodies
with whatever shred of faith
we have left in us.

Letter to Debbie from the Lincoln Park Zoo

Wolves don't have yellow eyes at all,
but golden brown like the buttered toast
we'd eat late morning after all-nighters.
I watch the lemurs wrestle, then stop
to groom each other at the top
of the swing pole. Remember how
we French braided each other's hair?
You showed me the way to brush
rouge on the apple of my cheeks, line
my eyes with black liquid liner.
We thought we were exotic, desirable.
The African lions lounge on concrete,
yawn at the faces pressed against
the glass, and the otters flip and scamper
as if content in the manicured riverscape,
recycled water, camouflaged walls.
But the wolves know what a cage is.
To them, walls smell like poison,
metallic and bitter as thorn.
They walk a groove into the carpet
of earth, conspiring for wildness
when or if it's ever needed again.
We circled the bars drunk
on attention, our legs long, our skirts high,
waiting for someone to love us back
into ourselves. We weren't picky.
We claimed we were happy behind
that fence built for girls like us, eager
for the rescue that never came.

Postcard to my Father from the Mojave Desert

I'm burning here. The back of my throat constricts,
and vowels come out like sand, easily scattered
but heavy when scooped and bagged. All the words
we strung on the line from home led me, sunbaked,
to this world of extremes. Hot days. Cold nights.
A silence so loud it fractures our vision until we
can't see ourselves or each other. The spines
of a barrel cactus spear my leg. I taste its flower,
the bloom of blood orange on my tongue, and spit
seeds to the wind. The creosote bush paints a shadow
for the scorpion and its poisonous claw. A diamondback,
camouflaged in pebbles, sips the air for a taste of prey.
The desert is thirsty, the sky an unbreakable blue.
Joshua trees spread stout arms upward, speaking peace
in whispers only bats can here. I look for little things
that color a world possible: a needle-splintered sun,
a pink cloud that proves nothing dies without first
folding its heart in surrender. The bats rise from the rocks
in one harmonious wave. They feast. The trees are praying,
still praying for rain.

Kitchen

He is making a sandwich,
dipping mayonnaise from a jar
with a spoon and spreading it
with a knife. You watch
his hands—strong hands—
and from this angle, maybe today,
kind hands. But you can't be sure.
You watch as he slathers
mayonnaise thick to every corner
of the bread, picks up another slice
and does the same. The spoon
and then the knife. The scoop
and then the spread. Methodical,
edge to edge. You are in the
doorway, frozen, spreading
your breath between minutes
so you don't risk startling him.
You are a child, but you know
the flash that lies between
a kiss and a curse. How quick it is.
He adds turkey to one side, layers
of turkey, then blood red tomatoes
cut dripping, warm from the garden.
He licks the knife, grunts.
You have perfected the art
of freezing like a fawn by instinct,
to slow your heart, to not blink.
He is eating. His jaw moves up
and down. There is a chance
for kindness, but with a little luck,
he will finish eating without seeing
you at all.

Unknowing

let it begin in the body   a shedding of sadness and skin
let the eyes be hollow   let nothing be measured in absolutes
run hands along your sides   and feel your ribs
a ladder that rises to the ledge   of your name
let it go—your name   it's not necessary to say
who you are   unlearn the cage you built
to keep yourself safe   say open
say soften   say yes

and let it begin in the dirt   of every thought that left you
unworthy of yourself   all skull and eye socket talk
of less and less than   all femur and scapula talk
of dark and darker   the everything you couldn't make happen
the nothing   you couldn't stop clenching in your fists
this is the meat   you grew up on
the stew of vinegar and salt   that made you pucker
and gargle and spit   there are rows of teeth
waiting to bloom like a lily   overnight luscious and pink
waiting to swallow a day's sun   in one gulp
say ready   say here

and let it begin in the breath   it's not the same thing
as forgiving   there's nothing to forgive
this is the distance you've traveled   the white space
between words   what you've said
what you're about to say   what you can afford to forget
because it's not a debt   you carry anymore
it doesn't pay   for the bones in your hand
all reaching for the bowl of your belly   ready to learn
how to ask for more   ask yourself what you need
from this world   say windows
say wings

III.

A Shadow Dance with Knives

How We Fit

There is no way to do this
except by lying
down, so we lie
on the bed and place
our hands on each other's
bones. Both of us
measure the truth.

There was a time I could wear
your jeans—you were so thin
and didn't carry the weight
of years, and I was
tall enough to fit
the length of you. You said
I was all leg and that was one
reason you loved me, and while
I appreciate your love
for how my legs wrap
around you, I need to say
we are both more
than our bones.

We stay in bed
marrow warm, and test
our spines, the sacral
and the cervical, the backs
of our heads resting
bone on bone, the blades
of our shoulders
the wings underneath
all we ever meant to say.

I Won't Call This a Love Poem

What is it you see in me when you steal
those glances, as if to look too long
might make you confess some secret

long gripped tight inside you?
And why is it that when you say
the word *love*, I see a flash of light

through the keyhole
of your sturdy, well-carved face?
For a moment I think you might

excuse yourself, leave the room
and shake out the bunched-up quiver
in your voice, but you swallow it back

and move on. To the soldier in you
who has known too much the death
of all that's fragile,

and the way any sign of weakness
can get your eye shot out,
I say, well played.

There are far too many flirtations
and love songs for any of it to mean much.
What do you say we keep hidden

our blue-bruised hearts? We'll be
anomalies, not saying our valentines,
not sharing our tentative trust.

If we're good enough, we can hold
this together for a lifetime, our friendship,
a shadow dance with knives,

our warmth bleeding each other dry.

Tattoo

I'm thinking about wings.
Kirk, the tattoo artist, draws bird figures
on a piece of scrap paper, asks me if I like them.
I'm thinking about herons. The big blue one
that stands knee deep in the Little Harpeth.
When it flies, it floats its legs on the breeze.
Its wing span, the length of my whole body,
casts a shadow even larger. I'm thinking about
air current and down drafts. The wings slicing
a path. I'm thinking about Kirk's ink and piercings,
his waist-length hair braided thick as rope.
He says it's easier to be still if I don't look
at what he's doing—which is needling my wrist
with a tiny pin that has the bite of a blow torch.
I'm thinking of black as it spills into my skin.
Black on white. Black in white.

When they hunt, herons stand motionless
but hear and see everything. They hunt alone.
The last time I saw one, it was standing on the eave
of our house, waiting to scoop the koi from the pond
we built together. Seeing everything. Hearing
everything. I'm thinking about wings. Kirk fills
them in on my skin with blackest ink. Black in white.
He talks about clean edges. His braided hair
hangs like a snake down his back. I'm thinking
about ink. I used to write your name beside mine
over and over to see how they fit together,
how they flew, the wings of the letters looping
towards each other and apart, and apart. We hunt
alone. The blow torch comes as a tiny pin, enormous
in shadow and seeing everything.

Two Halves Don't Always Make a Whole

Half kidding, half serious,
we tell each other *I love you*
then turn our heads to look
at something trivial, so we won't
need to explain those words.
I try to balance
on one leg just to see
if I can do it in this
half-drunk state.
The wind pouts
into a storm, one surge
and then another,
half cold, half warm.
You tell the story
of your cousin's wedding,
and the booze that made you
dance like a fool, and then
you show me
what a dancing fool looks like.
We fold ourselves over,
half laughing, half crying.
The mention of the wedding
sobers us
half freedom, half prison,
half passion, half terror,
and we stand still
and begin to think of lesser things
as if we forgot the words
we said earlier, which is just as well.
The half-light colors your eyes
moody and unreliable,
and my mouth
half smile, half frown,
can't speak above these feelings—
half anger, half relief.

Metro Station, Paris

What is love but a screech
of metal as the train begins to move
and the automatic door slides shut,
you behind it, me still on the platform.
You expected me to keep up, to follow,
and what is love but expectation—
mud-clouded as a spring river.
What a mess my heart made, quivering
in its drawer, and my breath, feathery
and slight. You gave me rules. You said
to think of you as a storm, heavy
with rain, to touch you when the moon
rolls to its side and lights the clouds.

Maybe I loved too much. In my defense,
I'll say I'm easily enchanted, drawn
by tides to confess my passion. I want kisses,
skin on skin. I want to whisper. I want to climb
dark stairs and find you shaving in front
of the mirror, the nick on your chin drawing
a drop of blood and that blood like a storm
in reverse. There's a rush of air on the platform
and someone sings a sad song in a pinched voice.
What is love but a series of missteps leading me
to an unlocked door? What is love
but the message on my phone, telling me
to take a train to the next station.
You're waiting for me there.

Between Us

It is February and the rain
that's been building the clouds for days

reaches a bursting just when
a wide arctic hand scoops low.

My southern town is pelted
with ice. In your northern home,

maybe you are sipping coffee
from the handcrafted pottery mug

you bought at the craft fair,
or making a sandwich, slicing tomatoes,

and thinking how less juicy and red
they are than ones from the farmers' market.

Maybe you hear on the Weather Channel
that the south is bracing for a fierce winter storm,

and already, cities as far
as Atlanta are seeing snow. Maybe you

remember I don't have chains
or snow tires and you hope I've been to the grocery.

You are fond of snow, or at any rate
are used to it and rarely notice the cold,

but maybe you recall me beside you,
shivering on a cool rainy spring night

and you regret that you didn't
put your arm around my shoulders,

offer me the elements of your affection
because fear and appearances got the best of you.

I hope if you are still standing
in your small kitchen alone, pouring

another cup, you remember
the time you touched my face when it was dark

and we held each other
much too long saying goodbye.

Maybe you think of me scraping
my windshield, slipping on my driveway,

my hands red and numb,
and wish you could warm me

in the cave of your arms.
Promise you'll breathe deeply the fragile air,

and check your phone
for my message, and send me a smiley face in return—

a small trade for these feelings,
too vast and desperate for the space between us,

and maybe
too beautiful for words.

Night in June

That night in June,
the wind charged with a threat
of storms, we sat on the steps,
our shoulders touching.
We spoke of solemn things
within the chorus of shadows
as fireflies emptied the dark.
You said you loved somebody once
like you thought it would surprise me,
and I said I'm afraid of drowning
and that tornados taunt me in dreams.
The things we shared were not expected—
patches of memory and mercies unwinding
into an awakening that scared us into silence.
We could have sat there for hours,
maybe we did, but rain moved in from the west,
unburdened the clouds and veiled us in myth.
We reached toward each other, but stopped,
resigned to feeling unsettled and guilty.
If I had known what to confess,
I would have told you all of it—
the nothing and the almost,
as the wet grass blew wild in the wind.

Letter to Andrew from Flagstaff

You haven't seen stars
until you stand under true dark
skies and watch a billion billion
needles of light prick the black.
I gape at the desert's rim and feel
like I'm floating into space,
my body a fragment of friction
and dust. I think of you, years ago,
in that damp basement where we
drank warm beer and danced
with people we said we didn't like.
I watched you kiss a girl—your mouth
on hers, your eyes on mine—and still
I remember how the hot center
of my belly burned, how the white stars
behind my eyes flashed like supernovas.
It was a game, you said, like so many
others in the years that followed,
ones that focused a narrow light
on our shadowy love. I lie on my back
in the sleeping bag and count
shooting stars—a fizzle and flash,
then gone. If you were here,
would you lean your face to the night,
point to Venus, Mars, Saturn's
spinning moons? Would you trace
the constellations, track them
till they fade in morning's pale glow?
I know the rules about letting go,
how loneliness is a plate of darkness
that must be consumed. I know this arc
of horizon is a rant of what-could-have-been-
but-wasn't, a celestial blast too wide to grasp.

It's the blackest space I've known, Andrew,
and with it, a silence that seeps into my skin
like a memory I can't see through.
I know I shouldn't miss you,
but I do.

Frost Flowers

They break when touched—

so delicate and temporary
we only harvest them with our eyes.

Hairline cracks in weeds bloom
an aura of bluish ice,

miniature glaciers inching
against the frozen grass.

Our breath is a curtain
we hide behind. In this field,

our suffering is white and hollow,
bitter in the space between us.

All night the world evolved
and we just sat there, waiting

for crownbeard and ironweed
to wind some brittle shard

of memory out of the sky
and spool it back upon itself.

Stems burst and ice pours out
in petals. Slowly, over the morning

we count the hours
and think ourselves lucky

as we stand in the curling dawn.
It really did

take this long.

The First Time I Ate Oysters

I found a pearl.
The smooth whiteness a rarity, an omen,
the gemstone of June,
the month of your birth.
The first time we met
        led to the first time
                we kissed, leaning against your car
in the cool midnight relief of a sulking summer.

The first time you bought me a cheap dinner at Applebee's.
The first time you bought sweet wine
and we drank it in the car
and drove home drunk and singing.
The first time I said I love you
                and didn't mean it.

The first time you met my parents.
The first time you said you saw my mother in me
                and it wasn't just the eyes,
which led to the first time we argued.
The first time
        I felt homesick for you
                the weight of it like a boot in the gut.

The first time I said I love you
                and was afraid to mean it.
All the times I admitted, if only to myself,
I wasn't sure what love was,
        what the big deal was,
                what the point was,
                        what the excuse was
and was this love
        and was I loveable
                and why didn't I feel loveable.

The first time I said I had plans that didn't include you.
The first time I learned pearls arise from suffering.
The first time I said all my plans included you.
The first time I said I love you
            and thought I meant it and was afraid to feel
                        this exposed, this vulnerable—
the way a pearl must feel
ripped
out of the oyster.

Split

With me you were different.
how your father's fist felt
you spoke in words
almost as if
of another boy
and did not wear your bruises.
At school, you bumped you
and wore the label
he'll never amount to much
That was when
The bad kids stood
waiting for the vice principal
and you took yours
to class unrepentant
Your eyes would find mine.
In our quiet moments
and you'd say *yes*
then *not really*
and calling me that night.
In the dark
of our telephones
as if I were the only person
For an hour or two
to be simple
before the fights and lies
In spring, during finals
I watched your shoulders
in front of me
you could hold the darkness
I wanted to give us both
School ended.
In the summer you slipped
into night.
toward other things

Even as you told me
against your face
soft as sighs
you told the story
one who was not you

pushed against the rules
kid who doesn't try
so why bother to teach him?
paddling was allowed.
in the hallway
to deliver *licks*
almost daily and came back
emotionless as a soldier.

I'd ask you if it hurt
then *not much*
then talk of shop class

between the lines
you'd tell me your secrets
you could trust.
it would be safe enough
before the booze and drugs
closed you again.

as you sat in the seat
and wondered how long
you carried.
the answers we needed.

away like a shadow
I turned
and didn't see you go.

If you asked me then
I would say *yes*
then *not really*.
Life fractured us.
into origami boxes.
and from each other
If you ask me now
I would say

if I missed you
then *not much*

We folded our bodies
We split from ourselves
like broken mirrors.
if I remember
all of it.

Pentimento

To revive the marriage, we
take field trips to art museums,
listen to experts expound
              genre and technique, explain terms.
The art historian traces
a faded image over the canvas—
a ghost sloop in the ragged sea
              sheered beneath blue foam,
white spray. Time raised it
from underneath, a memory
in oil blooming like invisible ink.
              Not a mistake, she insists,
as if mistakes
don't haunt even the most
pious canvases. A choice,
              a change of temperament,
a sudden sway angling away
from first course. We listen
to what she says about
              century-old pigments, chemical chains
loosening, dissolving, lifting
to light and air. Cyan, titanium,
umber fades to light, molecules
              blending oxygen and time.

              Only the impulse remains—
first thought that spurred action,
the human penchant for shifting
too strong to fight.
              What is permanent anyway?
In one painting, a Civil War soldier
turned farmer swings a scythe against hay,
the vision of those fatal blades
              biting the flesh of the past.

His face is shadowed,
and if there is repentance
only the painter knew for sure—
        his pent-up memento,
leaching through layers,
the underdrawing undoing
the desired scene. And in another—
        a farm yard with its dusty barn.
We study the lively chicken
while a phantom woman rises
beneath the color of dirt
        in carbon black pencil lines.
Who can say what she carried
beneath that layer of paint.
Who can know what she sacrificed
        to stay there.

Calligraphy

In winter, we see
the true shape of things—

the curve of one branch
wrapped around another,

the raw bones of rock
unmasked in dry grass,

the dark ink of nature
spelling bare words

on a white page—while
the syllables we keep

from each other
are wrapped in ice,

a hyphen between us,
camouflaged in trees.

Sun and Rain

after Natalie Shapero

Some people say sun and rain together means a wolf
is getting married and some say a jackal has stolen
the wolf's new bride. Some people say a bear,
all combed and bramble free, is memorizing his vows
and some say it's a donkey's wedding day. Some call
the rain noble and some call the sun a glitter ghost.
I want to marry the rain, bind it to me slick and bright,
but how long till I'm alone in knee-high grass?

Some say a tiger is marrying a fox and some say
the fox is taking a bath after eating paralyzed chickens.
Some say the wolf is taking the fox by the throat
and all those happy vows mean nothing at all.
Some say a cat is giving birth and a deer is giving birth
and a hyena is giving birth and the one-eyed jackal
watches in amazement. Some people say a monkey
and a donkey are getting married and they both carry

a key to the leopard's suitcase that holds his tuxedo
and wedding shoes. Some say the rain is naked
and the crow and fox are planning the organ music
for the processional. Some say orphans are crying
and the grandmother holds a handkerchief of shadows.
Some say the sun is lying, and the devil's daughter,
who looks a lot like me, is pinning a boutonniere
on the lapel of a dog. I say

rainbows are a lot like marriages and mirages—
it's just a certain light that makes them real. The fox
is blind and the crow circles low over the open field
while the gypsies dance with the devil's wife. The leopard
scatters petals down the aisle and the witch lights candles.
A ghost hides the ring in the pocket of his pants.
My husband, the rain, tells me he's leaving. The sun
pats dry my grassy tears. I am ready, dearly beloved,

for cake.

An Ending

Weren't we beautiful together,
our dark hair and blue eyes?
Didn't we see, for a while at least,
the need we each promised to fill?
Like a creek bed needs water.
Like a lung needs air. And didn't I
see the moment it shifted—the pause,
however slight, that portended
an ending? Didn't I let you say
what I knew was untrue? Didn't I
listen? Didn't I sit with you
until you were talked-out, wrung
like a sponge? Didn't I lift my face
when the room pressed down?
A screw tightening. A chain twisted
upon itself. Weren't we amicable
and rational, our words a mirror
of sane discourse until they were over
and you picked up your coat
and walked out the door? Didn't I
sit for an hour with my hands in my lap?
When I walked to the kitchen, poured
the wine down the drain, let the water run
and run, didn't I stand there
until every last piece of you drowned?

IV.

The Dark Lake

The Sex Life of Swans

In May, five to ten eggs. But first,
in February, a protective male, raging
as if some wild demon boils his blood.

He splits the lake as he charges through it,
neck back and eyes wide in red-wild ire.

We watch from our perch on the bench,
where moments before you felt the foot
of your son push out from the inside. You ask me

if it hurts to have my skin rearranged in such lopsided
ways, knowing we built this burden

in both of us, love and fierceness, and I said
sometimes it hurts
and sometimes it doesn't.

Sometimes it feels like I've waited forever for this
tumble-turn being with shudder-shifting feet.

The swans intertwine necks, breast to breast,
bill to bill, and he calms enough to see
the pink streak of dawn against a blue-black water.

The rage is just below the surface, a mirror image
of a frantic love, swirling among rushes at the water's edge.

In June, the hatching. But first, a protective passion
that matches what lies beneath your refined humanity—
the way you guard me and your seeded child

swimming in the dark lake, pressing
tiny footprints against both our hearts.

Eve Tries to Remember the Words to Hush Little Baby

After Abel's blood cried out to God
and Cain was sent packing, Eve stands
in the attic and goes through their things—
all the baby and little-boy-blue clothing,
favorite toys, and books she'd read at bedtime.
She finds Cain's blanket, ragged with love,
and remembers holding him in the rocking chair.
Hush, she sings, *Hush little baby, don't you...*
but has to stop for the tight clench around her neck
she imagines is God's curled hand. She tries
to let the music form inside her and float out
but can't remember what words come next.
Toy after toy, she grabs from the shelves—
Abel's dump truck and butterfly net, Cain's toy soldiers—
piles them in her lap until they cover her thighs,
her belly, until they are stacked to her breasts
and even then she keeps reaching. Her hands full
of marbles and legos and baseball cards,
Eve's throat burns. *Hush*, she croaks,
hush, hush, hush.

How a Woman Learns to Sing the Coyote's Song

Four children by three different men
and I'm here to feed them. The men

who laid their bodies on mine, how
long do you suppose they stayed, how

many nights have I spent listening
for their footfall in the wet grass? (Listen

to my baby's sigh, sounding just like
her father's.) I don't blame them, like

I don't blame the stars for shining
on a world they've got no business shining on.

This life is fact, plain talk,
not much hope—no way to talk

dreams without seeing the trash in the ditch
where the rainwater washes the ditched

desire for any good thing at all. Do you think
I didn't love them, that I was thinking

about holding something for myself, some beauty
from my body, like the hymn of a beautiful

memory or the tail of a wish sent spiraling
down from some unknown place, a spiral

as soft and dear as the hair of this child?
See the faces of my children.

Clean, every one, and fresh as pine.
I've no time to waste pining

for miracles—a little extra and space to breathe.
Those men were storms breathing

through my body, but the song you hear
around me now is the coyote's song,

as fierce and as cold as it's forced to be.
I will be what I have to be:

every morning a scavenger, every night
a lullaby of star-dipped nights.

Don't worry about us, we'll live.
I'll manage. I've done it all my life.

Love Poem

A child really can cry all night, her breath
wheezing and wrapped in wails, her red
newborn face gasping for its first brittle air.
No one mentions that it hurts to slice the lungs
with oxygen, that light glares cold and white.
I remember I held her and cried too, saying
everything will be all right. But tonight
I'm not sure I have the power to make anything
right for the now twenty-three-year-old face
pressed into my chest, this no-longer-a-child,
always-a-child face wounded by a serious wrong.

This is the night I stand on the porch
while the humid darkness swells
like some dead thing in water, and the film
in my throat is hot and curdled like milk.
This must be what drowning feels like,
lungs heavy as wooden oars.

Let me start again. A child really can cry
all night and I must let her, and let the words
I want to say crystallize on my tongue and dissolve.
Because the next breath will come hard
and I have to let it. Because the next moment
will settle like a leaden weight and I have to let it.
Because my words won't be peonies blooming,
or bluebirds slipping nimbly into flight,
and I have to let them be the hollow echo
of a hawk's hoarse cry and hope that morning
will come fast and brilliant and brave, and that love
will make some kind of difference in the end,
even though it doesn't, right now, it doesn't.

Austin

for my daughter

When I say Austin, I mean
the capital of Texas, the heat,
humidity, the bohemian-hipster vibe
you wore when you moved there.

I mean the street art, the color
in your face when you showed me
the postcards painted on the sides
of taco shacks and tattoo parlors.

I mean the tattoo on your shoulder
and the other one on your hip,
the eternal desire to take flight,
and the balance, to find center.

I mean the outlaw, the pain
you wore from a marriage of damage
and drought to a new home, a lone star,
a two-step not defined by violence.

And when I say Austin, you must know
how hard it is to let you carry
that faraway word beside your name,
to stand on the Congress Bridge

and see the bats stream like dark milk
into the deep unknown, to watch you
let go and dare midnight to stop
its curve into morning, shouting

you are no longer afraid of the dark.
I mean Mohawks and dog parks
and longhorns and food trucks
and Lady Bird Lake, which is really

a river skirting the heights, just like
Austin is really your wingspan,
your sparkler, your sky-stream,
your song no longer silent.

Memorial for Stephanie

It's a lovely bench. The dance
of the wood's burl spirals
like spirits. It's a sturdy bench—
handmade with thick varnish.

You probably know who trudged
the brambled forest with a burden
of love and set this spot as memorial.
The creek feeds the lake

and waters the blue larkspur
through summer's haze. The birch
shelters the chipmunk who tunnels
leaves and tightropes fallen branches.

The turtle sunbathes, the hawk
hovers over the lake's blue hollow,
and your bench is the respite
for those of us who bore this far

into the silence of ourselves.
Seventeen years—your life—
and you *lived it with joy*,
so announces the bronze placard.

You did well, Stephanie, despite the brevity
of your days. Many of us cannot say
as much, as we let despair wash over us,
allow dusk to gloom dawn.

Your smile will be remembered,
the bench proclaims. As I sit here,
I imagine it—unconquered, uncontained.
I can almost imagine I know you.

But maybe, in this hushed place,
I only know myself a little better.

Pomegranate

After the appointment, you shop for Persian rugs online and sip a glass of Bordeaux. The kind of wine a sommelier would swirl while he talks tannins, but you, who know little of blackcurrant noses and chalky edges, study the deep red gyration and imagine hula hoops and spirographs. You don't grin like you might have once. You are serious in your shopping. How to tell hand-made from machine-made. What the designs mean, delving deep into the symbolic, the sacred. The immortal peacock. The fertile pomegranate.

On this website alone, there are two hundred and seventy-two rugs with red as one of the colors. Red for courage. You learn that colors vary according to computer screens. It's hard to tell if reds lean orange or pink, if muted means dull, or vibrant means garish. It will matter when you lay it on your floor. It must be elegant with presence. It must be aged, well-balanced, dense with lovely structure. You shake your head. Swirl the wine. It coats the glass with vivid, dark cherries.

At the fertility clinic, the specialist said it was still too soon to give up. The ripe body surprises. And there are always options. Agencies and test tubes. Green and brown and gold. Double knots and Ankara silk blended with wool. Beautifully sweet and dark. You say the word, let your tongue wander along the sacred edges. Motherhood. Mother. The wine breathes on your lips. Red. Redder. The kind of wine a sommelier would swirl and talk mouth-feel, aftertaste. Symbolic. Intertwined diamond of male, female. It will matter when you lie on the floor. The crushing scent of fruit and soil.

Stillborn

I am
                an azure sky
sleeves of cotton
tied in knots
a spotlight
of push and pain
                and an echo
a name
the bowl of my belly
                breaks and crumbles
in slivers and dust
I watch the clock
as hours grind
and feel your small blue body
shudder in mine
                and I am
spreading out
pulled through time
like a ribbon
you are still
                a whisper
a memory
of your floating life
binding each bone
                delivered
in this breath
I hold your flesh
upon my chest, the hands
of the clock and my own
wrap you
this one moment
                alone

in space
in the cerulean, turquoise

        and terrible
sky

after miscarriage

after the blood
and the body's
surrender   after
the slow fold
of a living envelope
sealed and delivered
still   one more injustice
a metal scaffold
for your legs
medicinal purge
and scrape of all
the fractional flesh

what was left
inside you   you wonder
but a field of trampled
grass   torn sheets
wadded into ropes
wet rocks that held
starry cold

you shouldn't feel
anything   the doctor said
except a little pressure
and indeed the pain
stayed still and hard
in the back of your throat
like   an enormous
cackle, a sound
too high for human ears

what was left
                    but the bones
of a broken tree
the red fury of space
the cracked canal
of a pent-up river
with no way to reach
the sea

                spill
you thought
pound the noiseless shadows
until they sing
a requiem
Death is not a small thing

the doctor pushed back
let the nurses clean
your sunken belly
newly small
you'll feel better now
he said
we got it all

Visit from my Lost Child

When he comes, I am sitting on the fallen trunk
of a persimmon tree, waiting for the sun to carve
the mountains from the night.

I catch the scent of pine and smoke before I feel
his hand on my shoulder, before he traces the bones
of my neck and back with his thumb.

He unzips my skin, climbs in, wraps his arms
around my heart, presses down its beat. I feel
the urgent quickening of a newborn star,

the patient settling of a cradle. I tell him the mirror
shatters every morning, that my feet are paved in scars.
Every time I lift my head from the table of sorrows,

a crow pecks out my eyes. My heart pours oil
from its split chambers and he spins himself out of me.
He sews the bones of my spine with a fishhook

and red twine as the sun flings itself on the hills.
Stay with me, unborn flower, broken tune.
He fades at first light, once again too soon.

V.

Whatever Light Lies Waiting

Available Light

I've come to the lake to take pictures,
capture first light lifting off water,
         an image that is more
than the muted colors of a somber morning,
a world worn dull with sorrow.

It's hard to find a reason to smile
when all around me the edges of the good
         I believed in sink beneath a hard reality.
I can't argue that the world isn't sometimes terrible.
If you listen to its language, you stall beneath its weight.

But watch the lake. It wants nothing more
than to stroke the shore, curl kind arms
         around the sun-shifted bank.
The things I want are simple too—a fingerprint
on the window of understanding, a thread of faith.

It's not memory's work to hold me crouched
against the brick walls of my suffering,
         nor is it the will of my past
to latch the gate and leave my dreams starving
in the shadows of a narrow field.

The sun rises every morning—
the sun stands to speak at the lectern,
         sweating and brimming with light.
So what if my heart is broken.
That's part of a heart's job—to break

a thousand times over the darkness of this world
and still peer through the smallest window at dawn,
    ready to leap across the empty lawn
and gather whatever light lies waiting,
like manna, to fuel a single day's breath.

I take what I can—a spectrum of color
as photons dance in shimmering waves,
    the light brilliant and endless.

Blue Moon and Bright Mars

Now that I have you back,
even your early morning footsteps
seem blessed, and eggs scrambling
in the skillet, the aroma of relief.

I watch you from the doorway,
your clothes hanging on your body,
your hollow face busy in thought, until
your eyes lift and burn me with light.

We learned how to say love without words
when the hospital nights sank their teeth in
and the days chewed slowly on your flesh.
We learned how to say pain,

even the desperate kind that leaves you
rolled out flat and dirty.
And though we haven't yet admitted this—
maybe we never will—we learned

that fear sits in a sacred chamber
and uncoils the minutes of our lives
like the skin of an apple
peeling off in one long red helix.

Last night, we sat on the back porch
and watched the moon—a rare blue moon,
twice full in a month—curve
above Mars, low and bright.

To say your eyes are like stars is trite, I know,
but when I look in them I feel weightless,
moving fast across our lives,
the dizzying spin of all our plans bundled

like atoms in a molecule, barely contained.
We continue our habits, glad
for the repetition, the safety of the familiar.
Everything is the same,

except when you hold me and I feel the tremor
in your arms transparent as breath. It is no good now
to use words to explain ourselves, so we sit down
for breakfast. We eat our fill.

The Words We Feel

In jest you say *I want to die first,*
and it's almost as if you have. I want
to snatch the words out of the air
before they settle like a gravestone.

What were we thinking
when we pressed our bodies together
knowing there would be a day
one of us would be left behind?

What would I do
if thunder breaks the walls
and I have to bear the call of grief
with its loud and powerful voice?

Outside the wind pitches the evening
and the curtains fly like flags
from the open windows. We knot
ourselves to the ghostly air.

You say don't think of it but how can I not,
knowing what I know even as the mouth
struggles to say it. Once we were invincible,
but we are older now

and anything can happen.

Anniversary

The year finished the first slow circle
of missing you, and just as you predicted

the daffodils returned with a harvest of gold.
The hillside is ripe for gathering.

You waited until spring to die, until the earth
expanded to accept your body in a cradle of green.

Come back.

You've been too long gone and the ache you said
would ease, hasn't. The pangs you said would cease

wrecking the bright new joys of *without-you* days
still sharpen their teeth in the stillness of night.

What's not to like about returning?

The snow is gone and the koi are awake
flashing orange and white in the pond.

The path to the meadow that harbored
the small herd of deer needs clearing.

Trillium and bloodroot wait for your cry of discovery.
Peonies long for your bouquet.

I know you think I'm fine, that I haven't counted
each day as one more to endure.

Would you be surprised to learn I've forgotten
how to laugh, that winter left me unbearably cold?

I've done what you asked. I donated your books,
your clothes. I haven't missed a day walking the dog.

Come help me plant lettuces and tie the blackberries
to their stakes. Come pick out new roses to plant by the fence

as the daffodils spread tender yellow in the grass.

The Minotaur's Last Interview

I like circles, how each side sweeps behind me
to shake hands. I like the labyrinth, a path of circles
the mind makes during sleep. I watch the migration
of birds and know the moon will soon whisper

to nights stretched out like shadows, blue curves
on blistering snow. I learn what loneliness means
by the way my heart lurches at the sound of bullfrogs
singing on wet rocks. Everything I love is gone—

the larkspur that held the rivers in place, the frieze
of wild blackberries in the hills. I'm sorry I have no
anger anymore. The fire I had inside me became smoke,
became ash. I know that's less than impressive.

When I pray, it's like this: forgive, forget, forgive.
I can't think of a reason to keep praying. My soul
speaks out loud. It asks, *Who are you?* My body speaks
out loud. It answers, *Me.* So it goes—more circles.

Do you wonder what I do with my days? I balance them
on the tips of my fingers. Do you wonder what I do
with nights? I gather them with broken poems,
send them home on the backs of snails.

No more questions, please. No one needs answers
that float away like cottonwood seed. Here, take
the attitude of mourning and bow your head. Bind
the pieces of yourself like sticks tied with string.

When you write my story, don't leave out any part of it,
even the ending. Suffering doesn't have to be so formal,
or so restrained. The only thing left to do now is wait.
I won't remind you I never asked to be born.

There

My father hikes trails to get there.
Didn't matter if a storm loomed or daylight faded,
once he started, nothing could change his plans.
Rainbow Falls and Sweat Heifer. Gregory Bald and long
hard sections on the Appalachian. There was no dawdling,
no pause. Only steady onward progress. I learned,
in the struggle to keep up, to ignore the blisters
and throbbing muscles. I learned I was an inconvenience,
a waif behind his sturdy back.

I held the vistas as I walked,
the sunsets and breathless streams, glimpsing secrets—
a red mushroom, a spiraling vine, a wood thrush
camouflaged in leaves repeating its song. I kept these
for later. Holding my father's trail books, I fingered
the check-marks, the dates, restless treks that dog-eared
our family, crisscrossed our history.

There is an unmarked place
where the creek bends, where trillium and snowdrop lift
white and sacred from the dirt. There, the woodpecker
drills for beetles. There, the horned owl calls for dusk.
And there I stand in the shattering light of a falling sky,
the path splayed out in front of me like a scar.

My Father is the Poem I'll Never Write

after Cecilia Woloch

surely I'm not   the only one
who remembers   how tenderness
first bathed your face   a little bashful
like a preschool ballerina   at the recital
how it made you look   younger
and at the same time   fragile

children   shift your perceptions
and surely grandchildren   do the same
I watched you holding   your new granddaughter
and thought   who is this man

he never smiled at me like that

and some tiny part wanted   to snatch her back from the ruse
I watch you   now that another grandchild
joined that first one   and your face has grown
accustomed to   surrendering to joy
your large dark hands   weaving gentleness
your eyes crinkled   with kindness

and how they love you for it

you walk with us   to the new playground in the park
we let the children   run ahead
you slip   your hand in mine
and I feel   stung with grief
though I can't say   exactly why

I try to leave the past in the past
knowing we lived the same history but wrote
different books and no amount
of page turning will color it a fairy tale

you bear your tragedies and I mine

and both of us have regrets
both us of carried our heart like a stone
but maybe we've always been wrong
thinking we had to shoulder forever that weight
maybe instead we've been hollow
waiting for the right time
to be filled

A Small Book of Virtues

you said a dog
in pain knows no better
than to bite the one
that lifts its broken body
from the gravel, each pinch
of teeth a guttural grinding
against your forearm
and from you no sound at all

though we were only children
it seemed to us that the whole world
was held there dying
all at once in your arms
and as the back of your hand
wiped your cheek
and left a smear of blood—
the mark of a benevolent pain—
that we were witness
to something sacred
we could not name

Loving a Dying Man

You tell me you have come to a point
of acceptance, like stacking stones
for an altar, and there is nothing to fear.

I am afraid of hurting you, I confess—
your bones are so fragile—and you smile
before you calm me with your hands.

You tell me I carry love like I am solid
and whole—which is how it should be.
You hold love in your fingers and let it filter

like sand. You see its infinity and infirmity,
the base and the spire, the brave crest of it
and the secret cave. With your mouth

you tell me these things. With your body
you tell me you still depend on touch,
the rhythm of breathing, the scent of sweat.

This is what we understand. This touch now.
Which is how it should be. Which is the way
we will love each other the next time, and the next,

and the last.

Hypnosis by Landscape

From what I remember, there was a clenched fist of root
and stone, and a cactus with the slanted face of a cougar.

There was dirt on my hands and sand in my mouth.
My arms bronzed to burnished copper.

I walked alone, listening to the moon's tenor solo: *soon, soon.*
Lyrical wingbeats floated above me—a condor's dance.

When I stumbled on the uneven path, acacia trees held me
in their arms and fed me mesquite. I chewed the bitter meat

and swallowed a passion of wisdom and age. I tunneled warm
red earth with my hands, studied a gorge of river and rock.

The cliffs stood guard above me and flooded my face with grief.
The sun tossed shadows and I caught them in my teeth.

Lupine, paintbrush, creosote, poppy burned bright around me.
I stood in flames of scarlet and gold.

A meadowlark balanced on the saguaro's arm and sang me awake.
When I opened my eyes, the horizon called my name.

The Silence

Sit in the room with your mother and let the silence
that follows death sink in. Let it seep into your skin

so you'll remember every tiny tremble and fading rhythm
of the life that held your making. This is important.

Don't be scared.
Don't *not* look.

See beyond death's mask to what used to be,
so that what *will* be will not break you.

Don't close your eyes to the stillness.
Don't refuse to touch the cooling hand.

Little heart,
this is the desperation of man—past fire, past flood,

past the crackling crust of mountain and the soft whimper
of the vale. When you think about your own small life,

how it pulses in the room like a soundwave, you'll know
what to do with sorrow's song. You'll know to let the earth

speak loss—the making and unmaking,
the slow dance of tides.

Don't worry about the future, how you will face
tomorrow's black drape. You've witnessed the last breath

of the person who gave you your first.
Now, you know everything.

VI.

The Light Brilliant and Endless

Advice

My grandfather let it slip, like a joke,
that years ago in Widener's Valley,
back in that Virginia sawmill town,
Grandmother drove herself to the college
at Emory and had a conversation with the dean,
convincing him with Appalachian logic
to let her audit classes for free.

She soaked up the things they taught
like biscuits in sorghum, like beans simmered
in hog lard. In her stiff bodice and ebony skirt,
she turned away from the boys' snickers
and didn't lay her usual sharp tongue
to whipping those rascals. She held
her strong back straight, pointed her chin
to the purple clouds stewing over the hollow
like she knew something special
and would keep it safe.

When I got the nerve, I asked her why
she'd done that peculiar thing, and let slip
my secret wish to go to the college
in Jefferson City and learn my way out
of this mountain life. She patted my knee,
leaned into my shoulder, *You won't be
catching much of nothing chasing dreams
around here.* Then she stopped, blue eyes
long over the hills, her voice low as the whisper
I keep hearing on lonesome nights,
But child, you keep on chasing them anyway.

Sandy Coomer is a poet, artist, and endurance athlete living in Brentwood, TN. Her poetry has been published in numerous journals and anthologies, and she is the author of three poetry chapbooks, including *Rivers Within Us* (Unsolicited Press). Over 130 of her paintings have been published in literary art magazines, as well as being featured in local exhibits and art shows. Sandy is the founding editor of the online poetry journal *Rockvale Review*, the curator of the ekphrastic poetry project *20/20 Vision, a Poetic Response to Photography*, and the founder and director of Rockvale Writers' Colony, located in College Grove, TN. She is a teacher, a dreamer, an explorer, and an Ironman triathlete. Her favorite word is "Believe."